Sonnets & Sentiments

Audrey McHugh

Audrey McHugh

SONNETS & SENTIMENTS

© Copyright Pending 2018 by Audrey McHugh
With the Library of Congress
All rights reserved.

Paperback ISBN: 978-1723570872
Cover design by Audrey McHugh
Photos provided by Audrey McHugh

Published by PBJ Enterprises, Inc.
162 Liberty Street, Deer Park, NY 11729
United States of America
Email: walsh516@aol.com

Printed and bound in the United States of America
First Edition

Audrey McHugh

CONTENTS

Audrey McHugh
Graduation from Kings County Hospital
1956

ABOUT THE AUTHOR
Audrey McHugh

I was born on July 4th, 1936 in Brooklyn, New York, the third child in a family of seven to Austin and Olive Owens. I went to our parish school, St. Sylvester's, where my favorite subject was History. My sister, Gert, became a nurse and I followed in her footsteps at Kings County Hospital. At night, I studied English literature and Art at Hunter College. After graduation, I married my sweetheart, Charlie, and in five years we had three beautiful children.

When our youngest, Thomas, was four years old, I returned to work part-time. All these years later, I can still remember their wailing, "Mommy, come back!" as I walked to Lakeside Hospital in Copiague, Long Island.

I have been a camp nurse, school nurse and industrial nurse at Fairchild Republic. My life has been busy with work, church, family and travel, but always making time for reading and art. I have been writing poetry for many years. It is only recently that I have edited and organized my poems.

For what they are worth, dear reader, you be the judge.

The Author's Parents

Austin Owens   Olive Ryan Owens

Audrey McHugh

DEDICATION

To my children, Elizabeth, Joseph and Thomas,
The beauty and fulfillment of my life's work
Who have conquered mountains, natural and emotional.

To my grand-daughter, Kathryn, truth be told
In whose company may I never grow old
In gratitude for the happiness she has given me.

To my son-in-law, Tony, the music-master
And all around Sunday task-er
Thank you.

In loving memory of Diane and Charles,
To have and to hold from this day forward
And forever in our hearts.

Diane McHugh   Charlie McHugh

Audrey McHugh

PREFACE
By Audrey McHugh

My family is Irish Catholic, so there was always a lot of talking and praying at our home. My mother, Olive Ryan, was born in Newfoundland, made our clothes and played the piano. My father, Austin Owens, was an artist and prodigious reader. Many of his books are on the shelves in my dining room.

My high school, Wisdom Academy, closed in 1980 and we were invited to take books from the library. I have two Shakespeare volumes circa 1901 and thus began a lifetime love of poetry and the English language. Last year I took my granddaughter, Katie, to the Globe Theater in London. I wanted to acquaint her with "The Sweet Swan of Avon" (William Shakespeare).

My husband, Charles, our children Elizabeth, Joseph and Thomas, and I moved to Babylon Village on Southards Pond thirty-five years ago. All adults now, they are my happiness and inspiration. Charlie's grave is on the other side of the pond. I see him in my memories eye, true to his Franciscan calling, casting bread upon the water. Last winter, I saw a graceful egret, poised motionless, frozen in time. Another winter, I nursed a great blue heron his dying breath fading into a frosty  mist. My muse is all around me. May it be ever so.

I have travelled extensively, coming to realize that the journey of everyone's life is fulfilled in faith, family, country and art. When we fall short in the giving, there is nothing left but forgiveness. I have been writing poetry for many years. I am touched by the beauty of nature, the kindness of strangers and the parade of life that is ours for the asking.

PUBLISHER'S COMMENTS

Audrey McHugh's book of poems is a treat for all those who love and appreciate poetry. As I read her gifted words, something quite surprising and wonderful happened. I found myself traveling back in time as her words opened the doors of treasured memories in my own life. In those special moments, I magically relived precious times of love, peace and happiness with loved ones ... including some who crossed the life-line ahead of me. In so many ways, Audrey's book was such a pleasure to read. I trust you will have a similar experience.

Bob Walsh, Publisher
PBJ Enterprises, Inc.
Deer Park, New York 11729

Audrey McHugh

FAMOUS POETS ON POETRY

"A Midsummer Night Dream"
And as imagination bodies forth
The forms of things unknown, the poet's pen.
Turns them to shapes and gives to airy nothing.
A local habitation and a name.
William Shakespeare

"Heart-leap Well 11"
To freeze the blood I have no ready arts:
'Tis my delight, alone in summer shade,
To pipe a simple song for thinking hearts.
William Wordsworth

"The Task"
I am nae poet, in a sense;
But just a rhymer like by chance,
An'hae to learning nae pretence;
Yet, what the matter?
Whene'er my muse does on me glance,
I jingle at her.
Robert Burns

FAMOUS POETS ON POETRY

"Hudibras 11"
But those that write in rhyme still make.
The one verse for the other's sake;
For one for sense, and one for rhyme,
I think's sufficient at one time.
Samuel Butler

"Smart Set"
Poetry's essential character lies in its
Bold flouting of what every reflective adult
Knows to be the real truth.
Henry Louis Mencken

"A Defence of Poetry"
Like a poet hidden
  In the light of thought
Singing hymns unbidden
  'Till the world is wrought
To sympathy with hopes
  And fears it heeded not.
Percy Bysshe Shelley

FAMOUS POETS ON POETRY

"To the Earl of Roscommon"
Till barbarous nations and more barbarous times,
Debased the majesty of verse to rhymes.
John Dryden

Writing Free Verse Poetry
Writing poetry in free verse is like
playing tennis with the net down.
Robert Frost

Audrey Owens McHugh and Al Owens
At Ken and Lyn's Wedding
Vermont – August 2000

"A Brothers Epitaph"

I knew you, as the song did say

When hearts were young and gay,

And as they broke and sometimes lay

In the path of castaways,

To rise again and love repay

Nevermore to drift away

Or call to me and simply say

'Let's meet for lunch today.'

God sends his hope to keep at bay

The mortal wounds of life's decay.

He emblazons your epitaph on a rainbow's ray

To read 'Be love as it may'

May the arms of the angels hold you fast,

As your presence fades away

To a place where grief may never last,

And nature can't betray,

Where suddenly you will feel the rock

That holds our feet of clay.

Black Dome Roof

"A Mind Descending"

Her prime of life, in bitter black abides,

Mind unravelling, falling by the wayside,

Wounded, cherished daughter of our member

Did once elicit comments from aside,

Knowing well she surely was our pride.

Amber eyes once in gaze so tender,

Nevermore in life to see the splendor,

Staring with a look so wild and wide

Moving tears I never tried to hide.

Only child of love we shall remember,

Daily pray that this is just December.

Courage springing daily from the tide,

Giving us the strength to stand beside,

Hoping providence one day in pity send her

The crown and beauty being of her gender.

Robin and Wren

"Blindness"

Oh travesty of vision, seen again

Through groping hands that can't remember when

They last preformed as yours do now behave,

My talent lost that day among the brave

Fallen comrades, curse what might have been.

But here today I am for mortal men

A symbol of our triumph o're the grave,

Maimed instincts for the gold with which to pave

And shadows seen now two score and ten

Imagined as the robin and the wren.

Audrey McHugh

Memorial to Swiss Guards killed by Napoleon
Switzerland – September 2014

"A Soldier's Grave"

The last full measure

Well and good,

Pledged and given

As he should

Falling bravely

Where he stood,

Bleeding, dying

Pray he would,

Keep his treasure

If he could,

Death unbidden;

Soldierhood.

Elizabeth, Joseph and Thomas
At home at East 51st Street, Brooklyn, New York
1965

"My Children"

Their childish laughter through the years,
Fulfills my heart's desire,
My way of knowing danger fear
And worries dark and dire,
Unknown to them it would appear;
Of life they never tire.
My wild embrace will burn and sear
Consumed with holy fire,
All gathering to hold them near,
All loving to aspire
To give myself and dry their tears
And emptiness desire.

"The Sinai Seven"
At the summit of Mt. Sinai – August 2012

Father Michael Kerrigan (third from left)
Audrey Owens McHugh (on far right)
With fellow climber friends

"Climbing Mt. Sinai"

We ventured out at midnight,
And began to climb in haste.
Full moon our only guiding light
Into this desolate place.

Casting shadows in the dust,
Fearful that I might,
Fall behind, I know I must
Keep them all in sight.

Stumbling on my eyes adjust;
As years ago when in their flight,
Moses cursed them in their lust,
Carving idols their delight.

Ascending to this splendid sight,
A summit climbed in Godly height.
I raised my arms and piercing thrust
Myself into his love and trust.

Thomas McHugh
New York City, New York
2013

"Danny's Return"

In Limerick where once I did stay,
At the end of a very long day.
'Tis I from the states
Who's forgotten the dates
When loved ones sailed off on their way
Since you've forgotten my name
And late to the banquet came
Sure the truth must be told
Be it ever so bold
Let's drink to what I became
In billy club blue, a sight to behold
I've wedded a lass, to have and to hold
Loving in sunshine, never grow old
Down the streets that are paved with gold.

Babylon Beach
Babylon, Long Island, New York
2014

"Dawn"

Run barefoot by the shore with me
And smell the ocean air
Fragrant blow alive and free
Wildly in our hair
Rolling sea and cresting waves
Crash without a care
Upon the sandy beach foresee
It's bounty waiting there
As laughing seagulls boldness be
Our lunch picked clean and bare
All dancing in a symphony
And salty taste as fair
As any chorus you'd agree
With nothing left to spare
Turning round, look east and see
The morning sun's first glare
Shining "What I do is me"
'My warmth is meant to share'
As rays of golden yellow stare
At nature nourished everywhere.

Gerald Manley Hopkins[1]

---

[1] **Gerard Manley Hopkins SJ** (July 28, 1844 – June 8, 1889) An English poet and Jesuit priest, his posthumous fame established him among the leading Victorian poets. His manipulation of prosody (patterns of rhythm and sound used in poetry) established him as an innovative writer of verse. Two of his major themes were nature and religion.

Thomas McHugh and Diane Trentalange
Wedding Day
August 11, 1995

"Growing Up"

We have a son, who's grown to be

So much more that one can see;

In little ways that boys are said,

To bear their wounds with tears unshed.

Saying prayers at mothers knee

After "Old Black Witch" and "The Piglets Three,"

My Tommy Tucker blessed his head,

And years went by in a life that led

Down the fragrant path of a flower bed,

Into cub scouts and altar boys,

Of hockey games and winter sleds.

As he made his way so grows the tree,

Strong and true to all it's said

As his love for Diane on the day they wed.

Diane, Katie and Tom
Beth and Tony's Wedding
June 21, 2009

"Diane"

How can she be dying
Sweet presence resigning
The light of this day
Just took her away
Our tears and our sighing
Loud voices denying
Cries pleading we pray
'Not her, not today'
So silent, but trying
Forever abiding
When we lost our way
One morning in May.

Diane McHugh
St. Joseph's Cemetery
Babylon, New York
May 11, 2010

"The Funeral"

In dark despair we hurried faster,
Our mingled tears of stain,
Bearing grief in death's disaster
To question who is sane.

No more to know her joyful laughter
Or love from which it came,
No happy home for days hereafter
No sunshine in the rain.

We came to ask our prayerful pastor
She suffered not in vain?
And is she with our loving Master
And does she feel our pain?

Elizabeth McHugh Demarco
Wedding Day - June 21, 2009

"Elizabeth"

In the attributes of goodness

Laurel crowns her head.

Sweet beauty's best in giving,

By bounty we are fed,

Hands to hold in coming,

Gifted we are led,

Spirit land in blowing,

Loving kindness wed,

Daily prayer all knowing

Leaving none unsaid.

Wedded life all showing

Beatitudes well read.

Elizabeth at Phelps Lane
Babylon, Long Island, New York
2006

"The Feminist"

"A rag, a bone and a hank of hair"[2]

What a monstrous phrase for a sex so fair.

Rather vanity thy name is man,

Stole a kiss and away he ran.

A word to the wise is female perfection

Or risk sudden death and utter rejection.

Hurray for us! the brave and the true

If only our numbers weren't so few.

Down with men, so weak and so solemn

Afraid for the day we form a fifth column.

Your days are numbered, so watch and beware

Soon the law of the land will be made by the fair.

---

[2] ***"A rag, a bone and a hank of hair"*** These words are in Rudyard Kipling's poem, "The Vampire." An English journalist, short-story writer, novelist and poet, Kipling is regarded as a major innovator in the art of the short story, and his children's books are classics. He was one of the most popular writers in the British Empire in prose and verse in the late 19th and early 20th centuries. In 1907, at the age of 42, he was awarded the Nobel Prize in Literature. Rudyard Kipling (December 30, 1865 - January 18, 1936).

Audrey McHugh

Italy, near Lake Como
1995

"Eden"

He left the garden against his will,
If not for him we would be there still.
The lonely living in succession
Grasped for sustenance possession,

Forgetting that in fond affection
Love demands our self-defection.
If all in one will share the blame
Mankind's loss will be our gain.

Ascending as the phoenix brave,
Transformed and rising o're the grave,
Encounter life anew and deeper
To truly be my brother's keeper.

Audrey McHugh

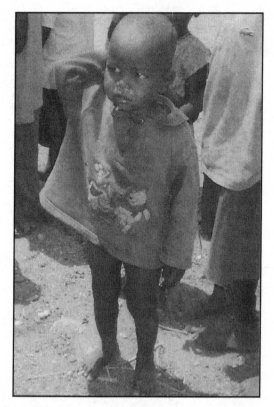

Child in Kenya, Africa - 2006

"Famine"

We traveled far, in spirit fed,
Challenged in a foreign land.
Famine's curse, nearly dead,
Battle brave, begging hands,
Grabbing hold, sadly said
'Help' into the searing sand.
Burning on as we were led
Across the fields of Africa
Watching as they bled.
Down the path of loneliness,
Lost innocence and dread,
In the land of aids and orphans,
Where life and death are wed.

Soldier's Memorial
Babylon Village, Long Island, New York

"A Soldier's Prayer"

A soldier prays in the midnight air,

He needs strength in his despair.

Thankful for safety through the day,

Hoping the morrow keeps dying away.

Many times it came near

So close he could hear

And each new disaster

A fear he must master.

He is resting now, his day's work done,

Hours and moments, passed one by one.

But if before dawn, he should draw his last breath,

The sleep that he takes be the long sleep of death,

Forgive him this day for all the blood spilt,

The centuries of orphans, widows and guilt.

Mt. Pilatus, Switzerland
2014

"The Cross"

Jesus tormented, messiah given
Bleeding and beaten with whips,
He rose in a Garden of Eden
And died with your name on his lips.

Born with my face before him
In a moment when time began,
Alien to pride and self and sin
Cursed by his fellowman.

We came to the cross, hoping to win
But away we also ran
Seeking repentance, that's never been
To shame me as I am.

Audrey McHugh

Tulip Bud
23 Pond Place, Babylon, New York
May 2018

"Creation"

In primordial time before history
The will of God did say;
Creation is our crowning
Let us make night and day
Earth and sky to overflowing
Sun and moon a world away
All rushing and unending
With life we can't repay.
From mountain lakes to goldenrod,
Lambs and lions where they lay,
Remaking how He loves us
In the budding month of May.

Audrey, Beth and Charlie McHugh
Home at East 34th Street, Brooklyn, New York
1963

"Time Passing"

If ever there was one as fair,

Nature proved in grace so rare,

A soul more given to this hearts care,

Love more constant than light and air,

A time for sweethearts to ensnare

Two loving hearts were beating there.

Waiting for one day to tear

Asunder what they cannot bear.

Diminished time will not repair

With darkness dwelling everywhere.

Ground Zero
September 18, 2001

"Honor"

If all the world in my hand held fast,
And the wealth of every glow,
Honor still outshines, outlasts
The substance of a rainbow.

It is ship to mast and stern to bow
So far and near to thee endow
When ages past meet years ago
Washed clean at last, we feel its flow.

And when time brings a last repast,
Making life seem long ago,
Standing tall and free at last
I trust but now I know.

Honor is our grace to grow,
A blessed bell and light for show.
Daily lived and future past
The only thing that lasts and lasts.

Audrey McHugh

Flowers at 23 Pond Place, Babylon, New York
2018

"Spring"

Oh can it be that white as snow

Has given up to better show

How crocus sweet and dainty grow

Upon the frozen ground bestow

A pasture verdant green aglow,

A better life, more than we know,

Of hope and love and future past,

Of many years before the mast.

May time again to all outlast,

A Spring to break our Winter fast,

Of days despondent, darkness cast.

Jerusalem, Israel

"Futureland"

The lion lamb makes ever more demands

To chose which face our brethren daily scans.

A driven darkness, all will surely shun,

Or mercy's mantle, smiling, duty done.

Graced with beauty, loving motherland,

Brothers willing, walking hand in hand.

Nature waits this rising of the sun,

Man and beast agree it's time has come.

Cresting waves breaking on the land

Crash its bounty beauty in the sand,

And living, dying, all have just begun

Our future and our past has been well won.

May time and telling help us understand

This greening of ourselves and native land.

Audrey McHugh

Pinelawn Memorial National Cemetery
2018

"Arlington"

Soldiers here at last are free

Stripped of life's vitality.

Their tombstones stand in morning dews,

As if in death they may refuse

All of life's adversity,

And winning immortality

Transformed into sweet purity,

All knowing life so suddenly

Is etched in stone as R.I.P.

4th of July Parade
Southampton, Long Island
1990

"Limelight"

You can't go home again they sigh,
Mother can't sing you a lullaby.
And seldom seen is foe or friend
To ease the pain or kindly lend
A welcome hand, remember why
I left, because I'd surely die,
My broken heart would never mend
Unless man to my talent rend
Applause and admiration sigh
Awards and honors, how they lie.
All too soon the road did bend
Leaving me bereft to fend
The silence that alone knows why
Success and fortune say good-bye.
But heart is home if I but tend
To wait and see what is godsend.

Nativity Scene at St. Francis Church in Manhattan

"Refugees"

Where is the promise of this land

When sad eyes gaze with open hand

Unknowing that it's all in vain

As the mother's womb from whence they came.

All laden with their life they stand,

The sentinels as the grains of sand,

And mortals wait in cold distain

To gather up their last remains.

Ruins of Towers with Banner on Pole
Three weeks after 9/11.

"Suicide Bomber"

A millstone in a hateful heart
Is all it took that day.
The conscience of his better part
Grown cold and cast away.
He called out "How great thou art"
No answer came his way,
When life and limb are blown apart
While children are at play.
May sorrow now to us impart
Our search for God and pray
Move dark despair to light of day
With love to make it stay.

Audrey and Frankie
May 2018

"Frankie"

Children now are gone and grown

But Frankie loves me best.

He comes and goes and brings his bone

And dances at my request.

He rocks and rolls at the doorbell's tone,

Putting courage to the test,

Afraid to come in when all alone,

"He only barks in jest"

Staying free of the danger zone

So giving up the quest,

Frankie and I, home sweet home,

Settled down to rest.

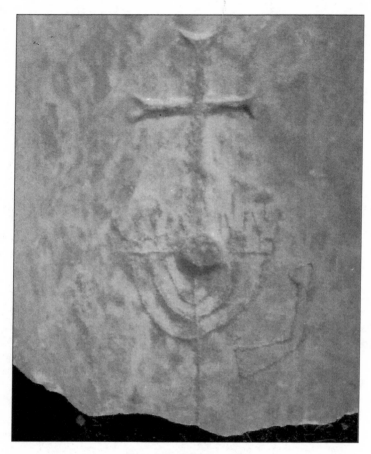

Cross and Menorah
Stone ruins in Turkey 2011

"Onward"

Read "Virtue is its own reward"
And "Blessed are the poor"
But they never bring you bread and board
Or make the cannons roar,
And surely as the eagle soared
It wasn't to adore.
Doubting can I now afford,
Neglectful, meet my Lord,
Surely he will ask for more
That never did give before
Faithfully in life accord
Forgiveness be my last reward.

Old Graveyard in Wales

"Bereft"

Women of old, not knowing the cost

Gave of their substance, loved and lost.

Like drifting sands on a windy day,

Built not to last is nature's way.

When I think of tomorrow, what life has in store;

Empty it seems, and what's it all for?

My future grows dimmer with every word,

Dying, pursued by a mocking bird.

In black borders, buried deeper

Inscribed, "To be my brother's keeper."

Audrey McHugh

Workmen in Turkey
2011

58

"Khomeini"

Our noble banner waved unfurled
Until one day in anger hurled.
Trampled in the muddy sod
Fanatics all, none spared the rod.

On one and all the dervish whirled
Excepting not the boy or girl.
Their leader with a hateful nod
Raised his fist and tied them hard.

Bound hand and foot the rope was curled
We're told to make a better world.
Anarchy reigns with knife unshod,
All praising in the name of God.

Maureen Murphy and Audrey Owens McHugh
Echo Lake Country Club
Fran Bradley's shower
July 19, 1993

"Good-Bye"

My childhood friend and confidant,
A touchtone felt so near,
The loss of life's communicant
In times of hope and fear.

We cry aloud as death is sent
'Not now, not her so dear,'
The sound is sad and dissonant
And unheard it would appear.

'My lifelong friend,' she said and meant,
Sweet words for me to hear,
But all the same I miss her so
Though smiling through the tears.

Remember when we came and went
Not seeing all as clear,
Or knowing that this last event
A loving heart may sear,

Enabling days that we are lent
And blessing time, in love repent.

Southlands Pond, Babylon, New York
2014

"Unbound"

I'm alone in a world of a thousand delights

As only a woman can be,

When the sweetest love on her heart alights

As the wind on a rippled sea.

My spirit soars to amazing heights

And amidst the galaxy,

Untouched by fear, in darkest night,

Unbound in time set free.

No obstacles to mar my sight

For in this company

Here you are, the brightest light

Aglow around and through me,

Warding off our unknown frights

Through clouds we cannot see.

I'd rather you than 'Midas mites'

Or power to foresee,

Or all the wealth of 'Arabian nights,'

For what are these to thee?

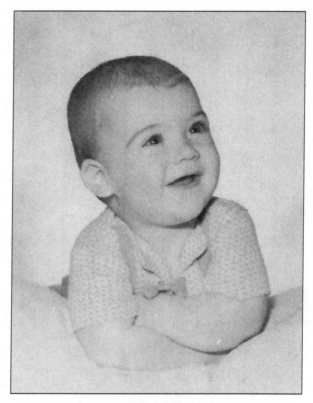

Joseph McHugh
Home at East 34th Street, Brooklyn, New York
April 1964

"Awaiting"

The days, the months, they come and go,

And still from him all blessings flow

The gift he will to soon bestow

Enchanting in our life to show

One blessed boy in bright blue bow

Whose time has come and yet not know

Whether happiness or life of woe

A shining face in heavens glow

Or fateful faults to bring him low

When winds of war and peace do blow.

As time awaits, a world below

All longing for our little Joe.

Beth and the Bishop at her Confirmation
St. Matthew's Church - 1976

"The Bishop's Late"

The Bishop felt our indignation
Sixty minutes in preparation.
Awaiting on his by and by
House rules here do not apply.

The best looked on in agitation,
The worst frowned in condemnation.
Singing out in weak reply
Chorus by the altar sighed.

Prayers rang out in supplication
Duty done in resignation.
Blushing in the moment fly
Never hearing where or why.

Presents

"The Gift"

A gift was sent but never came

For friendship sake it's all the same.

A time to give for heaven's sake,

A time to leave but not forsake.

A time to pray his holy name

Thankful for what he became.

The gift in which we all partake,

Our image in his own remake.

Forgiveness, though I am not to blame,

May it ever be our only aim.

Teresa Martin
Southampton, Long Island, New York
2013

"Death"

Farewell my friend,

You've taken leave,

And I am left with the bereaved.

Mourning, sorrow, comfort send

Missing you will never end.

Oh sweet life, with us weaved,

Loyal friendship, daily cleaved

Withered as I last believed

A loving God or faith's miscreed.

Charlie and Audrey McHugh
At Home, 23 Pond Place, Babylon, New York
2002

"Speechless"

Would that I had words to say
All things, all thoughts in such a way,
And let you know it's always time
To tell you that your plans are mine.
But words are weak and break apart
Except when written on a loving heart
So let me say again sometime
Words that I have never put to rhyme
But kept within the safest place
That ever love did care to grace.

Audrey and Ken Owens at Jackeline and Anthony's Wedding
Malverne, Long Island, New York
2009

"Ken"

I see him in my memories pain
That day so long ago
When all was new and unexplained,
Because we loved him so.

His boyish tousled hair did shine
In sunsets golden hue.
A face of innocence sublime,
And splashed with freckles few.

His pants too big and hitched too high,
A basket by his feet to lie,
A kitten in his arms to show,
A loving life for well we know.

Standing there for all to view
God's grace, God's child forever new.
I catch my breath, how could he die?
Choking tears to say good-bye,

As wind and rain comes passing through
Leaving life to start anew.

Dome of the Rock, Cross and Flag
Jerusalem, Israel
2008

"Failure"

He was my song and Sunday best,

Now gone and broken like the rest.

A marriage that gave up the quest

Of years when both held to a dream.

And is fulfillness just a scheme

To rob us of the proper stage

Whereby love protects old age,

And seek a more enhanced vocation

That time will prove cheap imitation.

Until we find ourselves still bound

Together in a lonesome sound;

Standing in utter loneliness,

Seeking God's forgetfulness.

Audrey and staff at Avalon Gardens
Smithtown, New York
2002

"Liberation"

Do you think it's time to go
Back to work, I mean
I've still my little Tom in tow
And Joseph's just been weaned.
To Beth I would deal a heavy blow
Come home sight unseen
From classroom in the second row
To empty house, I mean
Bereft of Mothers love to show;
Their source from all blessings flow.

Charles and Audrey McHugh
Wedding Day - May 13, 1961

Tom Gorman, Connie Nolan, Charles McHugh, Audrey Owens McHugh,
Gertrude Owens Bradley, Maureen Murphy, Barbara Koch

"Loving"

Gentle and low, in the afterglow,
Soft words for me to hear,
Embracing arms, entwining flow,
Forever hold me near.
Would that I may never know,
In keeping life so dear,
The loss of it, as time bestows
Loves glory to appear.
Looking back at years ago
Hoping one day to be here
I'm kissing you to better show
Love's whisper in your ear.

Church of the Nativity
Bethlehem - 2010

"Christmas"

Once upon a midnight clear,

Born again in life so dear,

A child would grow to banish fear,

His beating heart, for all to hear.

For David's star and manger mere

Did shine and from a babe appear;

A promise he will burn and sear

To hold us fast and draw us near.

Pinelawn Memorial Cemetery
Long Island, New York
2006

"Leaving"

I found your gold medal last night,

The one I put away,

Thinking of the day when you might

Come home again to stay.

I wept and remembered that lonesome sight

At the train when I heard you say;

Don't worry mom, I'll be all right

And if world and man betray,

Or the darkest dawn dims the light,

I'll come home, I'll find a way.

True to your word and wartimes' blight

In the graveyard where you lay,

Home at last, free at last,

You have finally found the way.

Area in St. Joseph's, Newfoundland
near site of Olive Ryan Owens' home.

"Newfoundland"

Author's Comment: I don't know if you are aware of the heroic behavior of the people of Gander, Newfoundland on 9-11. They are portrayed on Broadway in the play "Far and Away." They sheltered thousands of people, and their pets, when their planes were not allowed to land at Kennedy Airport. My mother was born there; our family returned there for her during the summer of 2018.

Seeing the land of my mother's birth
Walking the hills she roamed,
Hearing the source of her Irish mirth
On the road that took her home.
This is the sea, for all that it's worth
Twisting and raging foam,
Holding Titanic beneath deaths' dirge
Muffling the souls we still mourn.
These are the rocks that cling to the earth
On which many a man felt his rebirth,
Where even the skies came to bemoan
The Towers, the terror, as the world groaned,
And Gander rose up, in God given grace
Abiding with us in this hallowed place.

The above schooner is similar to the "Bonnie Lass" and another schooner which crashed on the rocks of Trepassey Bay on September 24, 1916 taking the life of Audrey's mother's Uncle Mike McDonald, 59, and seven others including his cousins, Peter and Richard McDonald (34 and 36), their friends Edward Grace (28), Richard Grace (36), Michael Grace (38), Edward Fagan (22), and Harry Lewis (27). They had sold their catch of cod and were headed home; however, with no ballast in the hold, a sudden storm swamped the vessel and claimed all their lives. Their bodies were never found.

Trepassey, Canada

Trepassey is a small fishing community located in Trepassey Bay in Canada on the southeastern corner of the Avalon Peninsula of the province of Newfoundland and Labrador. Trepassey originates from the French word trépassés (dead men), so named due to many tragic shipwrecks that occurred off its coast. Trepassey Harbour is where the flight of the "Friendship" took off with Amelia Earhart on board, the first woman to fly across the Atlantic Ocean.

"Trepassey"

The "Bonnie Lass" sailed on and o're
The restless sea and oceans roar.
Braving rocks that came too near
To tear apart the lives so dear,
Swallow ship and all she bore,
As many a man has gone before.

The waves rose up to burn and sear,
Their frightened faces to appear
Yelling, praying, limbs were tore
Asunder, as they asked for more
Mercy in this life of tears
Pity for the children dears.

Courage, suffering all they bore
Passing into loves' folklore,
Sinking in a watery bier
To fill the ocean with our tears
Longing still their jib to draw
A Westward wind and safety's shore.

Audrey McHugh (Nana) with Katie
At Beth and Tony's Wedding
June 21, 2009

"Katie"

At Southard's Pond, to the bridge we went
Though it was getting late,
To sail our sticks, broken and bent
Downstream to their fate.
Precious time that we are lent
Remembered at this later date
"Nana, where is the sunset sent?"
And "Why do fish need bait?"
Explaining what she really meant,
And nature needing no debate,
We fed the ducks and off we went
Suppertime for me and my Kate.

Charlie's Grave at St. Joseph's Cemetery
Babylon, New York
January, 2018

"Forevermore"

As Autumn leaves have lately cast
Their lot with the driven snow,
And sails are stripped from before the mast
As was done since long ago,

I like to ponder seasons past
Recalling all I know,
Of someone dear whose love did last
As long as God's winds blow.

If all the world in my hand held fast,
And the wealth of every glow,
All wishing him in heavens vast
Eternity bestow,

Peace and joy to ever last
And, Oh so long ago,
In hopes and dreams
Home at last,
Forevermore to know.

Prometheus Statue at Rockefeller Center
January 1978

"Ice Skating"

I'm having loving dreams of late
Like one described below;
Of you and I at a rapid rate
Circling an 'eight' as we go.

You were spinning on silver skates,
And mine had a golden glow.
Unknown melodies whispered our fate,
Heard through the drifting snow.

Listen my dear, time can wait,
The sound of the song, gentle and slow.
Lovers are patient at heaven's gate
Yours to know, Mine to show.

Charlie and Audrey at Tom's house
July 2004

"Charlie"

As I say good-bye to him
My weary saddened eyes do brim,
With tears unshed and feelings deeper
Than life and love to every seeker,
Who gives and takes a heart to win
While time its beating days do trim,
To make my life forever bleaker
And no more my dear ones keeper.

As snow falls white and sounds grow dim,
He goes to God, set free from sin.
The years did make his pride the meeker,
Imposing strength and voice the weaker.
And yet I find my strength in him
A hand to hold, and life begin.

Trees and brambles at Southard's Pond
Babylon, New York - 2003

"The Way"

When everything was quiet
I wandered on the way.
Stumbling in his footpath
I struggled there to stay.
Rain washed out his footprints,
Scattered rocks in disarray,
Faith gently took my hand
And led me, since that day.
Past pain and doubt, awakening,
Through love and loss to win;
When grace intrudes, forsaking,
All my selfish heart, remaking.

Firemen's Memorial at Babylon Village Hall
Babylon, Long Island, New York

"Virtues"

What is it that this love of mine
Is searching to foresee?
It is no secret so sublime
To hide from you and me.

Charity will stand the test of time
With the strength of the cedar tree.
Hope is a light that will always shine
With the power to foresee.

But above all else is love's binding vine,
Faith is my gift to thee.

Audrey McHugh

Southard's Pond - 2008

"Widowhood"

I thought I heard his voice today,
Though it was very dim,
Sweet words of care and missing me
So I knew it must be him.

I thought I felt his hand today,
Strong in his loving touch,
Leading to a better day
Of letting go and such.

I thought he blew his breath today,
Upon my tearful face,
Keeping sorrow sad away
And leave without a trace.

I thought I saw his face today,
Reflected in the light,
Beckoning, and come what may,
Abiding through the night.

Baltimore Oriole

"Saved"

A fleeting glimpse, a flash,

An avian orange oriole

Raids a squirrels cache.

In crispy leaves he forages,

Picking clean the stash.

This migrating boreal visitor

Then invades my trash.

Full and fed its' morning meal

Favorite is my citrus pealed.

Startled by my coffee crashed

Flees when squirrel makes a dash.

Cross Topiary

"The Coat"

He asked me in this season
Of days grown cold and gray,
My coat would be a blessing
Well what was I to say?

His face and hands were testing,
My life had gone astray,
But his was sorely pressing
To end in death that day.

I helped him in his dressing,
This coat my last display
Of former life successing
Now poverty at bay.

My mind daily distressing,
And hope a world away,
Less time in time possessing
Or, my faith in life repay.

In memory of the "Duck Man"
From the staff of Birkshire Nursing Home
2007

"Remembrance"

My broken heart despairs of ever knowing

Once again, and present in his coming

Joy and woundedness combined, forever showing

That life is all of these and even more bestowing

Times precious gift, confined but ever flowing

Loosed from its bonds and evermore becoming

Abiding love in winds of spirit blowing

Rushing past our coming and our going

Transforming all to fullness overflowing.

Majestic Mountains

"Forgiveness"

Sorrow upon my heart doth lay,

I know not what to do,

When friends say things they'd never say

If we hadn't forced them to.

All is out in the light of day,

Shame and sorrow to betray.

Forgive me, come and show the way,

The grace of friendship, born anew,

Enduring all, and come what may

Soul to soul and through and through.

Vanderbilt Planetarium
Centerport, Long Island, New York
2015

"The Tree of Life"

The Tree of life has many branches,
Some for the sick and lame,
Wild Winter wind enhances
The glory of its' fame,
In love and loss it still advances
Sometimes in deaths domain,
Dappled green the sunlight dances
Washed in Springtime rain,
Unknowing of its' call to answer
Or the source from which it came
Obliging it to tame and master
It's life, it's roots, it's pain.

Jesuit Cathedral, Lucerne, Switzerland

"Confession"

Bless me father, in his holy name
And the prayers that many I've said,
For all the years of pleasure and pain
When by darkness I was led.
As night and day were all the same,
In sinfulness and closely wed,
Useful as ill-gotten gain
By our passions we are fed.
Sacred sacrament for the maimed
Contrite as I bow my head,
Wishing hope is not in vain
Or forgiveness for the dead.

Court of the Patriarchs
Zions National Park
1999

"Stars and Stripes"

Wave for freedom n're to end,

Without it we must surely rend

The honor of this promised land

Enduring all but still demand

The teeming shores a right to send

Those 'huddled masses' to defend,

A destiny in fact so grand

Fulfilled we never may disband,

As red or blue, bowing bend

Band of brothers end to end

Together in a final stand

The rock of ages in our hand.

Katie, Audrey and Tom McHugh, and Johanna Pulis
Paradise Island, Bahamas
May 2018

"The Dolphin"

Awesome as he swam around

Rushing in a phantom chase,

Holding hands we fearsome bound,

Salt water left it's taste.

Responding to a slapping sound

And stepping up the pace,

He leaped above, rose unbound

Airborne in freedom's face.

Crashing down and coming round

Then fade without a trace,

When back he comes, in play rebound

To welcome our embrace.

In tears of laughter, falling down

Into this sacred place,

Holding on, with fear replaced,

Sweet Nature comes as grace.

Holocaust Memorial
Jerusalem, Israel
2008

"The Master Race"

Dark days spawned the master race
When cowards from the battle reeled,
Preferring more a paper chase
Than bleeding in an open field.

Nevermore or long deface,
With duty done and honor sealed,
Undaunted by the human waste,
Or the bells for whom they peeled.

The phantoms slept at Patton's base
While tanks upon the beaches wheeled,
And finding man's perverted taste
House to house did make him yield.

The sorrow of the human face,
Our common bond and common shield,
As if we ever may erase
The open wound that will not heal.

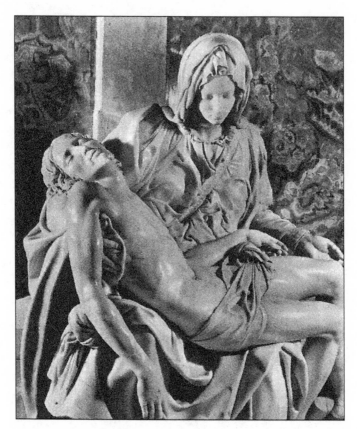

Pieta in Rome, Italy
1995

"The Labor of Living"

The wild Winter wind
Blows onward its uncharted course,
As life and limb to it must bend
Or surely may forever rend
The peace that makes worthwhile the cost
Sustained or be forever lost.

I look for comfort, not regret,
Missed calls, misjudged, in doubt beset.
Honor meant for courage send
Misused in thought that cannot bend.
Conflicted winds are tempest tossed,
Making war 'till all is lost
As 'win or lose' will soon beget
The carrion call 'till all is met'
Remorseful may forever fend,
Better now to make amends.

American Eagle

"The Carrion Call"

High on the wing

The eagle sings,

Over the land of the brave.

Gazing below at everything

Nothing escapes the grave.

O'er mountain and sea the carrion fling,

Consumed with nothing to save,

For nobility has a hallow ring

And shallow 'long may she wave.'

Grand Canyon, Arizona
1999

"Transformation"

When daffodils shall bloom no more,

And earth's sweet smell more pungent store,

Her water trapped and substance poor,

And wind withheld as gone before,

And rocks break down in every pore.

Will Nature lose the clothes she wore

Bereft of green and golden shore

And nevermore to be adored

Will earth and sky and spirit soar.

Transformed to be our evermore?

Statue of Liberty

"Huddled Masses"

They came upon a midnight clear
Quietly so none could hear.
They travelled long, both far and near
Heart in hand, the darkness fear.

Rushing in it would appear,
The torrent took the lives so dear.
Borders crossed, by starlight steer,
Tempest tossed on a watery bier.

All that's left, a child so near,
Washed ashore with many a tear.
Past time to see or voice to hear
Past heart to mend, or grace to sear.

The lonely living we endear?
Or huddled masses buried here.

Audrey Owens McHugh
Red Sea, Israel
2008

"Future Time"

Past all the years that I loved best,

Giving and taking as they passed

Aware of leaving my last bequest

And worldly wise in darkness cast

With open arms I made the quest

Forgiving what I had been asked

Not knowing if I passed the test

Or what day would be my last.

Faithfull knows, abiding lest

Daunted we give up the task

Of living life at His behest

Rewarded with a life recast.

Southard's Pond
Babylon Village, New York
1993

"The Test"

The test of time is every man's consent
To bear the blows, emerging still unspent.
Through ages past in truth it will be said;
Bind up your wounds, for him you have scarcely bled.

The night will come when darkness fuses dawn,
Assembling all the loveless and forlorn,
Whose life and limb are valued not as gift,
But chance encounters, man and beast adrift.

The mourning dawn descending dark as death,
Naked and alone in all we are bereft.
We crush the wretched phoenix on our breast
For rising from the ashes in her quest.

And sucking, swaying, sinking down in sin,
Our pleading voice bemoans what might have been.
If all mankind could breathe in heavenly praise,
By faith endure in love 'till end of days,

What if one day in time and tide ahead
Our earth and heaven pledge 'to thee I wed,'
And evermore embrace 'sweet beauties best'?
Then seeking, striving, winning past the test.

Melting Mendenhall Glacier in Alaska

"As long as I live, I'll hear waterfalls and birds and winds sing.
I'll interpret the rocks, learn the language of flood, storm and avalanche.
I'll acquaint myself with the glaciers and wild gardens,
and get as near the heart of the world as I can."
John Muir[3], explorer and conservationist.

---

[3] **John Muir** (April 21, 1838 – December 24, 1914) Known as "John of the Mountains" and "Father of the National Park," he was an influential Scottish-American naturalist, author, environmental philosopher, glaciologist and early advocate for the preservation of wilderness in the United States. His letters, essays and books describing his adventures in nature, especially in the Sierra Nevada, have been read by millions.

"On Ecology"

"Eulogy for Chief Seattle"
By his son, James Seattle

"Your time of decay may be distant
But it will surely come. Every part
Of this soil is sacred to my people
Every hillside, every valley, every plain and grove
The very dust upon which you now stand
Responds more lovingly to our footsteps
Than to yours and our bare feet
Are conscious of the sympathetic touch."

Quotes by Chief Seattle[4]

"When the green hills are covered with talking wires,
And the wolves no longer sing,
What good will the money you paid for our lands be then."

"The white man will never be alone.
Let him be just, and deal kindly with my people.
For the dead are not powerless."

"Man did not weave the web of life,
He is merely a strand in it.
Whatever he does to the web,
He does to himself."

"Take nothing but memories,
Leave nothing but footprints."

---

[4] **Chief Seattle** – Born in 1786, he was a Chief of the Duwamish and Suquamish
Tribes. Baptized "Noah" into the Roman Catholic Church, he was a leading
figure among his people who spoke in favor of protecting the environment and
respecting the rights of his people. The city of Seattle in the state of Washington
is named after him. Chief Seattle died on June 7, 1866.

Audrey McHugh

Farewell from Audrey McHugh

As in the words of William Shakespeare ...

"Farewell"
From Sonnet 104

To me, fair friend,
You never can be old.
For as you were
When first your eye I ey'd
Such seems your beauty still.
William Shakespeare

Audrey McHugh

REFLECTIONS

I have known Audrey Owens McHugh since the fall of 1950 when we enrolled as freshmen at Our Lady of Wisdom Academy in Ozone Park, New York.

Audrey was always possessed of an inquisitive mind and blessed with a superior intellect. She is a gifted artist who provided many of the illustrations for our high school yearbook. She made friends easily and kept them, as is demonstrated by our friendship of sixty-eight years duration. She enjoys, and is knowledgeable about, the works of Shakespeare.

She has travelled extensively, and, if you were to ask her where she has been, she more than likely would respond with, "It's' easier to tell you where I haven't been."

Well rounded, well-travelled, fascinating story-teller, talented artist, dedicated to her religion, excellent company – that's Audrey!

Veronica M. Boland, Esq.

Mrs. John Boland

REFLECTIONS

The first time I met Audrey I had just moved across the street from her. I was introduced by my teacher. She told Audrey to take care of me. Audrey was in the 4th grade and I was in the 3rd grade.

We went to the same grammar school together, high school together and played together almost every day. After high school, Audrey went to nursing school and I went to college.

I was an only child and Audrey had two boys and five girls in her family. I felt I had a large family to share my joys, weddings, graduations, births, get-togethers, sorrows, and life in general.

God bless,

Barbara Koch

REFLECTIONS

Mom always said my legs would carry me around the world. Years of playing hockey in our backyard had given me stout calves, I guess. Back then, neither of us could have imagined our going around the world together decades later: hungry grizzlies pursuing mountain goats in Glacier National Park; Northern Lights dancing overhead on the frozen Canadian tundra; a cheeky lone wolf trotting by us in Yellowstone; and, Grandpa's house nearly unchanged since the 30s in Catskill where he met Nana and made it all possible.
  Joseph McHugh

My grandmother is a woman of wit, wisdom and strength. She has the courage to be kind and laugh with the fullness of her spirit. She is an incredible writer and an incredible soul.
  Katie McHugh

My mom is the absolute rock of our family. She has been there for Katie and me in our times of need. She has boundless energy that rubs off on everyone in the family. She has omnipresence in our family that gives my siblings and me a feeling of closeness.
  Thomas McHugh

She takes me on a journey and leads me to the light of my life. She gives guidance and knowledge of the world which in turn makes me think and care about all people. As she lives her day to day life, she adds pounds of love to my life.
  Elizabeth McHugh DeMarco

PHOTO MOMENTS IN TIME

Al Owens, Gertrude Owens Bradley, Audrey Owens McHugh
Eleanor Owens Montgomery, Nancy Owens Rentz
Adele Owens Farley, Kenneth Owens

At Fran and Tom Capotorto's Wedding
Colonia, New Jersey
August 1993

PHOTO MOMENTS IN TIME

Charles McHugh (standing)
Veronica McHugh Dixon, Helen McHugh Nolan
Emily McHugh McCarthy and Clare McHugh Lagamasini

At Tom McHugh and Diane Trentalange's Wedding
August 11, 1995

PHOTO MOMENTS IN TIME

Our Lady of Wisdom High School Reunion
Port Jefferson, New York - 2004

Clare Sullivan Lee, Ronnie Maloney Boland
and Audrey Owens McHugh

June McGowan and Sheila Mahoney Brown

PHOTO MOMENTS IN TIME

Barbara and Peter Koch
And Charlie McHugh
Lifelong Friends
July 2004

PHOTO MOMENTS IN TIME

McHugh Family Reunion
Bridgehampton, Long Island, New York
August 2004

PHOTO MOMENTS IN TIME

Joe McHugh
Grand Staircase-Escalante National Monument, Utah
2012

PHOTO MOMENTS IN TIME

Joe, Tom, Katie, Audrey McHugh
Beth McHugh Demarco and Tony Demarco
July 2015

PHOTO MOMENTS IN TIME

Owens, McHugh, Rentz and Farley extended family reunion
23 Pond Place, Babylon, New York
July 2017

PHOTO MOMENTS IN TIME

Beth and Tony Demarco
January 2018

PHOTO MOMENTS IN TIME

Katie McHugh
At St. John the Baptist Choir Concert
May 2018

PHOTO MOMENTS IN TIME

Thomas McHugh and Marie Labuda
May 2018

PHOTO MOMENTS IN TIME

Audrey and Joe McHugh
At Metropolitan exhibition of "Hudson River School"
January 2018

SELECT BOOKS
Published by PBJ Enterprises, Inc.
Available in paperback and eBook formats through www.Amazon.com.

"Miracles at Saint Anne's Shrine in New York City"
By Bob Walsh
This book tells of the miracles still happening at Saint Anne's Shrine in St. Jean the Baptiste Church in New York City. The story begins with Saint Anne's life from childhood and continues as mother of the Blessed Virgin Mary, and the grandmother of Jesus Christ. The many remarkable events described are strictly based upon recorded ancient history, Catholic Church traditions and visions by various saints.

"Precious Memories Forever"
By John Egner
This is a wonderful love story written by retired Long Island surgeon, John Egner, in which he describes the joys and blessings he and his wife, Patricia Marion Conroy, enjoyed over 60 years of married life.

"My Life of Miracles"
By Bob Walsh
Looking back from early childhood to present time, Bob Walsh provides a first-hand account, a peek behind the scenes, into the reality of miracles, God, the angels ... and the devil.

"She Ate Her Spinach!"
By Joe Pritchard
This is a touching, heart-warming, love story that describes the 60 years of married life Joe and Maddy Pritchard shared. Hand in hand, they served God, family and others in their parish of St. Joseph's in Babylon, Long Island, New York.

SELECT BOOKS
Published by PBJ Enterprises, Inc.
Available in paperback and eBook formats through www.Amazon.com.

"A Treasure of Smiles"
By Father Al Pehrsson

"A Treasure of Smiles" is a series of books and coloring books in which Father Al provides entertaining, thought-provoking cartoons that reflect human nature, our relationships with one another - and with God. Much of his inspiration comes from over 60 years of service as a priest in the Vincentian Order including many years in a leper community.

"The Day They Killed Jesus Christ"
By Bob Walsh

This book is written as if the reader is actually present to witness the disturbing, heart-breaking events of the passion of Jesus Christ as they occurred. The graphic descriptions are based upon information recorded in ancient history, the Bible, Catholic Church teachings, studies of the Holy Shroud, and visions by various saints.

Historic Books by Edith Ammons Kohl
"Land of the Burnt Thigh"
"The Sodbreakers"
"Woman of the Cavalcade"
"Denver's First Christmas"

Edith Ammons Kohl is an American heroine, one of the first brave, multi-talented women who helped settle America's wild, wild West. Each of her books captures the sights, sounds and exciting events as they unfolded. Writing from personal experiences, her brilliant craft of words describes the grueling, sometimes tragic realities endured by so many involved in the taming of our country's wild West. These historic books are a unique treasure for all Americans.

INDEX

Made in the USA
Lexington, KY
08 October 2018